101 Classic Jewish Jokes

101 Classic Jewish Jokes

Jewish Humor from
Groucho Marx to Jerry Seinfeld

Robert Menchin
Illustrated by Joe Kohl

LYONS
PRESS

Essex, Connecticut

An imprint of Globe Pequot, the trade division of
The Rowman & Littlefield Publishing Group, Inc.
4501 Forbes Blvd., Ste. 200
Lanham, MD 20706
www.rowman.com

Distributed by NATIONAL BOOK NETWORK

British Library Cataloguing in Publication Information available

The original edition was catalogued by the Library of Congress as follows:

Menchin, Robert. 101 classic Jewish jokes : Jewish humor from Groucho Marx
to Jerry Seinfeld / Robert Menchin ; illustrations by Joe Kohl. Memphis, TN :
Mustang Pub., c1998.
    95 p. : ill. ; 19 cm.
    PN6231.J5 M46 1998
    ISBN: 0914457888 (alk. paper)
https://lccn.loc.gov/97036233

ISBN 978-1-4930-7690-1 (paper : alk. paper)

♾™ The paper used in this publication meets the minimum requirements of
American National Standard for Information Sciences—Permanence of Paper
for Printed Library Materials, ANSI/NISO Z39.48-1992.

Contents

Jewish Humor

RUSSIAN BALLET, ITALIAN OPERA, FRENCH CUISINE, and... Jewish humor. The special gift of the Jewish people to find humor in daily life has been enjoyed around the world. Once the province of a small, tight-knit community, Jewish wit is now integral to American—and world—culture.

Interestingly, the Jewish affinity for laughter is a fairly recent development. For most of their history, the Jews were serious "people of the book" who considered humor sacrilegious and trivial. Their talent for and love of jest blossomed in the late 19th century and came to full flower in the 20th.

Many of the best Jewish jokes traveled across the Atlantic in the early 1900's and were carried through Ellis Island along with bundles of clothes and family pictures. Throughout the 20th century, Jewish humor found fertile ground in the growing mass media of America and enriched popular culture. In the "old country," the jokes reflected living with persecution, poverty, and anti-Semitism: "laughter through the tears." In the New World, the jokes became parables about "fitting in" and reflected the problems of assimilating in a new country with a new language and new ways.

With its rich cast of characters and subject matter, Jewish humor mirrors the concerns of the Jewish people: marriage, children, health, success and failure, and—the butt of so many Jewish jokes—doctors and waiters. Of course, these are universal concerns, and in their jokes Jews speak to an audience that cuts across generational, racial, ethnic, class, and religious lines. Remember the old advertising slogan "You don't have to be Jewish to love Levy's bread"? Well, you don't have to be Jewish to enjoy classic Jewish jokes. They're for anyone who likes to laugh.

✡   ✡   ✡

It's no exaggeration to call the 20th century the Golden Age of Jewish-American humor. All the elements were in place to make it so. A generation of American-born writers and performers, blessed with the right to express themselves freely, were able to combine the comic traditions of their foreign-born parents with the energetic patterns of American life. In print and in performance, their jokes, stories, and comic routines found a receptive audience. By mid-century, the droll, folksy humor of Mark Twain and Will Rogers began to yield to the more relevant, urban comedy of Groucho Marx, Mel Brooks, and Neil Simon.

A variety of platforms—books, theater, radio, films, vaudeville, the Borscht Belt circuit, records, and TV—launched Jewish humor into the mainstream of American life. Today, Jewish sensibilities are echoed in the language of comedy across America, from stand-up jokesters in nightclubs across the country to movie comedies and TV sitcoms. A recent hitchhiker on the information superhighway, Jewish jokes are now exchanged eagerly on the Internet.

Throughout this century, Jewish comedy talent emerged from many media:

❏ Vaudeville and burlesque provided a stage for the talents

of Eddie Cantor, Smith and Dale, andWeber and Fields.

❐ Broadway gave us Fanny Brice, Molly Picon, and Ed Wynn.

❐ Radio made Jack Benny a household name and introduced us to "The Goldbergs" and Burns and Allen.

❐ When television came along, Milton Berle dominated Tuesday nights in America. After Berle, Sid Caesar and his "Show of Shows," with the legendary team of comedy writers Mel Brooks, Neil Simon, Carl Reiner, and Larry Gelbart, ruled TV comedy writing.

❐ Comedy clubs and nightclubs featured Lenny Bruce, Don Rickles, Buddy Hackett, Schecky Greene, Mort Sahl, Rodney Dangerfield, Alan King, Jackie Mason, and Joan Rivers.

❐ The Marx Brothers, The Three Stooges, and The Ritz Brothers created classic motion picture comedies and paved the way for the madcap films of Mel Brooks and the witty satire of Woody Allen.

❐ And Jewish film stars like Peter Sellers, Walter Matthau, Peter Falk, Goldie Hawn, Bette Midler, Billy Crystal, and Barbra Streisand brought their laugh-getting shtick to the big screen.

✡ ✡ ✡

Though modern Jewish humor is significantly different from the wit of early Yiddish dialect comedians like Benny Rubin and Menasha Skulnick, there are interesting similarities. Their voices may be silenced, but the sounds of Yiddish, that rich, expressive language, peppers the English language. Just as bagels, a Jewish food staple, can now be found in groceries across the nation,

Yiddish words have become part of the English language: "Is that deal *kosher*?"..."Proposing a deal like that takes *chutzpa*!"..."He keeps messing with this deal, and I'm tired of his *shtick*."..."Get a courier to send the contract on this deal—don't *shlep* it." Further, the cadence, phrasing, and structure of the Jewish immigrants' speech have become familiar to our ears. Listen to the punch lines of the classic jokes—"So it's not like a fountain."..."On him it's becoming."..."You'll hear such a scream."..."On me you can't count."—and hear the echoes of Yiddish, the language of the ancestors of most of today's Jewish comedy stars.

✡   ✡   ✡

Jokes, and often variations of the same jokes, are told in every ethnic group. So what makes a joke a distinctively Jewish joke? For starters, a love of words and argument are major elements of Jewish humor. There's an old saying: "Three Jews, three opinions." (Of course, if one of them is schizophrenic, you'll have four opinions.) The storytelling tradition and a passion for dramatic exaggeration are the foundations of many Jewish jokes.

In Jewish humor we find *chutzpa* as well as the flip side of *chutzpa*, self-denigration. Sigmund Freud wrote, "I do not know whether there are many other instances of a people making fun to such a degree of its own character."

In this book, many jokes confirm Freud's observation. But the jokes of all ethnic groups exploit the foibles and characteristics of their own people. The fact that so many American Jews tell jokes about Jews is a reflection of Jewish comfort and sense of security in this wonderful country. A proverb in Ecclesiastes says, "A fool raises his voice when he laughs; a wise man smiles." Thus, the best

Jewish jokes tend to be those with an underlying wisdom that provoke a nod of the head and a knowing smile rather than raucous laughter.

Witty, brief stories or anecdotes that make a serious point are among the most prized moments of Jewish humor. Eugene O'Neill's four-hour play *The Iceman Cometh* is about the human need for illusion and mankind's quest to keep a "pipe dream" alive to survive. Now, listen to Woody Allen in the last scene of his movie, *Annie Hall*:

> *Woody:* "Doc, my brother's crazy. He thinks he's a chicken."
> *Doctor:* "Really. Why don't you turn him in?"
> *Woody:* "I would, but we need the eggs."

In just three lines, Woody Allen says as much about one's need for illusion as O'Neill's four-hour play. It's an example of Jewish humor at its best.

✡   ✡   ✡

No discussion of Jewish humor would be complete without reference to an area about 90 miles north of New York City in the Catskill Mountains—affectionately known as the "Borscht Belt." If New Orleans gave birth to jazz, the Borscht Belt gave birth to stand-up comedy. The Catskills catered to hard-working, middle-class Jews who took their two-week summer vacation at one of the many hotels in the area—Grossingers, the Concord, Tamiment, the Nevele, and others.

The Catskill hotels opened early in the century and flourished between World Wars I and II. They catered to the two major concerns of their Jewish guests—food and comedy. The food, including plenty of borscht (red beet soup), gave the area its nickname, but it would be just as appropriate to call it the "Comedy Belt." In their heyday, the hotels were rated by the caliber of comedy they featured. The Borscht Belt was the proving ground for many of the best comic talents of the century—Jerry Lewis, Mel Brooks, Rodney Dangerfield, and many, many more.

It's only natural that comedy about food and service was one of the mainstays of the area. Here's a classic:

> *Customer:* "Oh, waiter!"
> *Waiter:* "Yes, what's the matter?"
> *Customer:* "Taste the soup."
> *Waiter:* "You always have this soup. Today, you don't like it? Look, mister, you don't like the soup, I'll bring you another soup."
> *Customer:* "Taste the soup."
> *Waiter:* "You don't want the barley soup, OK. I'll bring you some matzo ball soup."
> *Customer:* "Taste the soup."
> *Waiter:* "All right! All right already! I'll taste the soup. Where's the spoon?"
> *Customer:* "AH-HA!!!"

This chestnut reflects a major Jewish characteristic—love of drama. Why not just ask the waiter for a spoon? Because there's no drama to it, that's why. Many consider "Taste the Soup" the quintessential Jewish joke because it beautifully illustrates the Jewish tendency to make a big production out of a mundane situation.

✡   ✡   ✡

Many of the best jokes in this book are the creation (and the loot) of the great Jewish comedians of our time. Their numbers are legion and their names are legend: Henny Youngman, Milton Berle, Jack Benny, Buddy Hackett, Joan Rivers, Carl Reiner, George Burns, Mel Brooks, Lenny Bruce, Jackie Mason, Red Buttons, Albert Brooks, Sid Caesar, Gene Wilder, Alan King, Jerry Seinfeld, Paul Reiser...and many, many more.

According to *Time* magazine, in the 1960's, when Jews made up less than 3% of the population, nearly 80% of the top comedians and humorists were Jewish. Today, the number of non-Jews and other ethnic comics has increased, but Jews are still over-represented on the comedy scene.

As other performers and actors did, Jewish comics adopted Anglicized names to enhance their careers. (On page 42, there's a short quiz to help you match your favorites to the names they were born with.) Today, with a more sophisticated audience and an acceptance of multiculturalism, few Jewish comedians and actors change their names. Comic Jerry Seinfeld has had the top comedy show on television throughout the 1990's, and it's simply known as *Seinfeld*—a no-nonsense Jewish name. Other successful comics who retain their original names include Paul Reiser, Robert Klein, and David Steinberg.

(And it's interesting to note that when a young, black female comic wanted to succeed in the comedy business, she changed her name from Caryn Johnson to Whoopi Goldberg.)

To all the great Jewish humorists of this century—from George Burns, born in 1896, to Jerry Seinfeld, born almost 60 years later in 1954—we owe our thanks for the laughs and for reminding us of the special quality of Jewish humor.

✡   ✡   ✡

Where do Jewish jokes come from? Who writes them and how do they circulate?

Jewish jokes seem to spring full-blown from the atmosphere and are carried like pollen to nightclub stages, club meetings, and telephone wires until, finally, everyone can say, "I've heard that one before." I know I have. I can truthfully say that although my father never told me about sex, he did not fail his parental obligation to tell me every "new" joke that appeared on the grapevine.

Consequently, at least half of the jokes that appear in this book were written from my memory. There is usually some slight variation from one version to another, but the basic joke was there all along. When asked where Jewish jokes come from, I can only shake my head and say, "I don't know. Weren't they always there?" (A Jew answers a question with another question.)

In this collection are 101—no, I forgot, for *you*, 106!—classic Jewish jokes. You've heard that joke before? It's likely. It's said that Cain killed Abel because he told him a joke he'd heard since childhood. People who make a living telling jokes will tell you that there hasn't been a new Jewish joke in 2,000 years—only old jokes revisited, revised, and edited. And, of course, new audiences.

Included here are dozens of "golden oldies"—jokes told over and over, which you'll receive sometimes with a groan and sometimes with a smile, but always, I hope, with delight at seeing an old friend yet again. These are old jokes, but like good wine, they have aged well. That's why they're classics.

The reader may notice the absence of ribald jokes. Like most ethnic humor, Jewish comedy has its share of "adult" stories, and many of the top Jewish comics built their careers telling jokes you wouldn't dare tell your children or your mother. Lenny Bruce, for example, a brilliant comedian and social satirist, ignored middle-American boundaries of good taste but remains an important figure in the history of Jewish humor. However, I found little, if any, vulgar or lewd subject matter among the Jewish jokes one might consider "classic." Another (and perhaps more honest) reason for the absence of scatological humor: I'm not comfortable with off-color humor in pursuit of a cheap laugh.

Though the jokes may have lost something in the translation from Yiddish to English and from the spoken word to the printed page, you should be able to see the fundamental reasons they have survived the decades and continue to incite mirth. And if you like these jokes and want more, there are many books on the subject in many languages, all of which make Jewish humor more accessible to everyone and help assure its popularity into the next millennium.

In any case, the next time you tell a joke from this collection—*and you will, you will*—feel free to create your own version, as millions have before you. Remember that saying, "Three Jews, three opinions"? Well, it could also be, "Three Jews, three ways to tell the same joke." It's a time-honored tradition: add a different location, a new situation, your own timing of the punch line—and the joke is yours!

The Jewish Family:
Husbands, Wives, Children, and Especially Mothers!

*"The gods gave man fire, and he invented fire engines.
They gave him love, and he invented marriage."*

*"I've been married for 30 years, and I'm still in love with
the same woman. If my wife ever finds out, she'll kill me."*

"Listen to me, Mr. Levy," the doctor said, "If you ever expect to
cure your insomnia, you have to stop taking your trouble to bed
with you."

"I know, but I can't," the patient replied. "My wife refuses to sleep
alone."

❖

A buxom blonde at a charity ball was boasting to a friend about her
new diamond ring. "It's the third most valuable diamond in the

world!" she said. "The first is the Hope Diamond, the second is the Kohinoor Diamond, and then comes this one—the Finkelstein Diamond!

"Unfortunately," she continued, "the owner of the famous Finkelstein Diamond must also accept the famous Finkelstein Curse."

"What's the Finkelstein Curse?" her friend asked.

"Finkelstein," the blonde sighed.

❖

In a small Jewish cemetery on the outskirts of the city, a man is mourning aloud "Oh, why did you die? Why did you die?" over and over again. A woman putting flowers on a nearby grave walks over and asks, "Who died, mister? A close friend of the family?"

"No, as a matter of fact, I never met him," the man says and begins to wail again, "Oh, why did you die?"

"If you never met him, why is his death so painful to you? Who's buried here?" the woman asks.

"My wife's first husband."

❖

Sam met his friend Morris on the street. "Morris," he said, "I haven't seen you in years. You look terrible—what's happened?"

"You won't believe," said Morris. "I got married three times in the last three years and buried three wives!"

"How terrible, Morris, how tragic," Sam said. "What happened?"

"Three years ago, I married this rich widow, and she died a month later after eating poison mushrooms. A year later, I met this wealthy divorcée, and she died a month after we married, again from eating poison mushrooms. Then last year, I married again, and a month later, she died."

"Don't tell me," Sam said. "Poison mushrooms."

"No, a fractured skull." said Morris. "She wouldn't eat the poison mushrooms."

❖

Mr. Feldman came home early and found his wife in bed with another man.

"What the hell are you doing?!?" shouted the irate husband.

"See," the wife said to the man lying beside her. "Didn't I tell you he was stupid?"

❖

During a long car ride, Uncle Sol is driving the family crazy with a continuous lament: "Oy, am I thirsty! Oy, am I thirsty! Oy, am I thirsty!..."

At the next rest stop, her son rushes out and brings her a large seltzer water. As he starts the car to continue the ride, the silence is broken by Uncle Sol: "Oy, was I thirsty! Oy, was I thirsty! Oy, was I thirsty!..."

❖

Mrs. Grossman instructed the artist painting her portrait, "I want you should put a gold bracelet on each wrist, a pearl necklace on

my neck, ruby earrings on each ear, an emerald tiara on my head, and, on each finger, a 20-carat diamond ring."

The artist was bewildered. "Why do you want to ruin a beautiful painting of yourself with all that stuff?"

Mrs. Grossman explained, "My husband is running around with a young chippie. When I die, I want her to go crazy looking for the jewelry!"

❖

At his annual check-up, Izzy is shocked to learn that he has contracted a deadly virus and has only 12 hours to live.

When he gets home, he tells his wife Sarah the sad news. Overcome with grief, she comforts him and says, "Honey, I'm going to give you a night you'll never forget!"

After making love with a passion they haven't felt in years, Izzy says, "Sarah, that was wonderful, marvelous! Can we do it again?"

This time it's even more passionate. Sarah is about to doze off when Izzy nudges her and whispers, "How about another one? Come on, one more time."

"That's easy for you to say," says Sarah, "You don't have to get up in the morning."

❖

In the middle of lunch, Mrs. Slotnik is interrupted by a committee of workmen who report that her husband has been badly wounded on the job and is in critical condition at the hospital. She doesn't say a word and continues eating.

They say again, "Do you hear what we're telling you, Mrs. Slotnik?

Your husband was hurt—he's in critical condition!"

"Gentlemen," she says, "I heard absolutely every word. And as soon as I finish this soup, you will hear such a scream!"

❖

Mrs. Cantor, a widow for over four years, sat at the water's edge at Miami Beach, bemoaning her lonely life. Next to her sat a gentleman in obvious need of some color.

Mrs. Cantor asked, "So how come you're so pale?"

"I've been in jail for 28 years," he replied.

"Twenty-eight years! For what?" she persisted.

"For killing my third wife," he explained. "I strangled her."

"What happened to your second wife?"

"I shot her."

"And, if I may ask, your first wife?"

"We had a fight, and I pushed her off a building."

After taking a few minutes to absorb the information, Mrs. Cantor leaned closer to the man and whispered, "So, that means you're now a single man?"

❖

Little Benny didn't say a word for the first six years of his life. On his seventh birthday, his mother made him a cup of cocoa.

Benny took a sip and suddenly said, "This cocoa's terrible!"

His parents were astonished. "Why did you wait so long to talk?" they asked.

Benny replied, "Up to now, everything's been OK."

❖

Sadie and Esther are sitting on the porch of their Miami Beach hotel.

"Oh, my God!" cries Sadie. "Look at that poor boy! Such a weak chin. His mouth is crooked. And look, his eyes are crossed."

"That boy," says Esther, "happens to be my son."

"Oh," replies Sadie. "On him it's very becoming!"

❖

Sylvia, a respectable widow, agreed to marry Mendele, the town *schnorrer*, only if he would stop begging and find another occupation. He agreed, provided that she went begging with him for one year. "After that," said Mendele, "I will find another line of work."

For an entire year, they went begging together door-to-door. At 4:00pm, exactly one year later, Mendele said, "The time is up at last. We are now through with begging forever!"

"Okay," Sylvia said, "but let's finish this row of houses first."

✡   ✡   ✡

A Jewish gangster escapes from a shoot-out with the police and staggers into his mother's apartment on the lower East Side. Near death and with a gaping wound in his chest, he gasps, "Ma, I've been hit!"

"Eat, eat," his mother says. "Later we'll talk..."

❖

Sheldon tells his best friend, "Every girl I bring home, my mother doesn't like. I just can't seem to please her."

His friend replies, "Keep looking until you find a girl who looks just like your mother. Then she can't find fault with her."

Three months later, Sheldon meets his friend and says, "I did what you said. I finally found a girl just like my mother—same height, same hair, same personality. She was exactly like my mother."

"So what happened?"

"My father hated her."

❖

Esther and Sadie meet on the boardwalk in Atlantic City. Esther asks Sadie, "So how is your son?"

Sadie shakes her head sadly and replies, "Awful! My poor son is married to such a woman. She has to have breakfast in bed, she has to have a mink coat…"

Then Esther asks, "And how is your daughter?"

"Wonderful!" Sadie says, beaming. "She's married to a marvelous man who serves her breakfast in bed, and he just bought her a mink coat!"

❖

Mrs. Schwartz was walking down Delancey Street with her two grandsons. A friend asked, "How old are your grandchildren?"

She replied, "The doctor is five, the lawyer is seven."

❖

A Jewish grandmother and her 14-year-old grandson check in at a large, expensive Miami Beach hotel. The bellman brings in two trunks and ten suitcases and asks if there is anything else he can do.

"Yes," she says, "Would you please lift my grandson out of the car and bring him up to my room?"

"Oh," says the bellman. "I'm very sorry. I didn't realize he couldn't walk."

"Oh, he can walk fine," says the grandmother. "But, thank God, he doesn't have to."

❖

The married daughter calls on the phone: "Hello, Ma?"

"Darling, is anything wrong?"

"Oh Ma, everything's wrong!" she wails. "Both kids are sick, the roof is leaking, the stove isn't working, and I'm expecting six friends for a Tupperware party at lunchtime!"

"Darling, don't worry. I'll take a bus into the city, and I'll walk the two miles to your apartment. On the way, I'll buy food for the Tupperware party, and when I get there, I'll take care of the children. I'll even make dinner for Sidney."

"Sidney? Who's Sidney?"

"Sidney, your husband."

"My husband is Isaac. Is this 834-6184?"

"No, this is 834-6188."

"Oh...does this mean you're not coming?"

❖

An El Al airline took off from Ben-Gurion Airport in Israel and head-
ed for Paris. The plane's intercom was open by mistake, and the
passengers could hear the pilot's every word as he chatted with the
co-pilot: "Well, now that we've taken off, first I'm going to have a cup
of coffee, and then I'm going to find that gorgeous new stewardess
and kiss her like she's never been kissed before!"

The stewardess heard the pilot's voice coming from the loud speaker, so she hurried to tell him that the intercom was open. When she
passed the second row, an elderly lady seated by the aisle stopped
her and whispered, "Wait, dear—let him finish his coffee first."

❖

Mrs. Finkelstein gave her son two beautiful neckties when he left for college. When he returned home on summer vacation, he wore one of the ties to show his appreciation for the gift.

Mrs. Finkelstein took one look at her son and asked anxiously, "What's the matter? The other tie you didn't like?"

❖

Because of financial hardship, Mrs. Cohen is forced to become a streetwalker. After her first day on the job, she comes home exhausted and hands her husband the earnings—$10 and ten cents.

"Who the hell gave you a dime?!?" her husband demands.

"Everybody!" she replies.

❖

"Mrs. Grossman," the psychiatrist explains, "there's nothing physically wrong with your son. But I'm afraid he does have an Oedipus complex."

"Oedipus, schmedipus," Mrs. Grossman says. "Just as long as he loves his mother."

❖

An elderly woman climbs three flights of stairs, opens an ornately carved door, and walks into an exotically furnished reception room that smells of expensive incense.

A gong sounds and a beautiful Asian woman appears from behind a

beaded curtain and asks softly, "Do you wish to meet with His Omnipotence, the Wise, the All-Knowing, the All-Seeing Guru, the Honorable Maharishi Fatah-Naru?"

"Yeah," says the woman. "Tell Sheldon his mother is here."

❖

Jewish Logic

*"If the rich could hire someone to die for them,
the poor would make a nice living."*

Mrs. Goldberg walks into a butcher shop and asks the price of a pound of lamb chops. "Five dollars," says the butcher.

"Are you crazy?!?" Mrs. Goldberg says. "Across the street at Schwartz, it only costs a dollar a pound."

"So go buy your lamb chops from Schwartz," the butcher replies.

"He doesn't have any," Mrs. Goldberg says.

"Listen, lady," the butcher says, "if I didn't have any, I'd sell them for a dollar a pound, too!"

❖

A group of American tourists at the tomb of the Unknown Soldier in Tel Aviv noticed this inscription on the tomb:

HERE LIES ABRAHAM SCHWARTZ.
DIED 1973 DURING ARAB-ISRAELI WAR.
A GOOD SOLDIER AND A GREAT FURRIER.

"What's this furrier business?" a tourist asked the guide. "This is supposed to be the tomb of an unknown solder."

"That's true," said the guide. "As a soldier nobody knew him, but as a furrier he was famous!"

❖

A new flood is foretold. In five days the rain will be incessant, and the world will be wiped out.

The Dalai Lama addresses the world's Buddhists and says, "Meditate and prepare for your next reincarnation."

The Pope holds an audience and tells Catholics, "Confess your sins and pray."

The Chief Rabbi of Israel goes on television and says, "We have five days to learn to live under water."

❖

Abramowitz met his friend Ginsburg and asked about his job at the circus. "It's terrible," Ginsburg said. "Morning, noon, and night I

clean up after the animals. The pay is lousy. I stink all the time, so people avoid me and I don't have any friends."

"There are plenty of good jobs around," Abramowitz said. "Why don't you get a better job in town?"

Ginsburg was outraged. "What, and quit show business?!?"

❖

A short, skinny Jew walks into a lumber camp looking for a job. To impress the skeptical foreman, he chops down a towering oak tree in 90 seconds.

"Wow! Where'd you learn to do that?" the foreman asks.

"In the Sahara Forest," he replies.

"You mean the Sahara Desert," says the foreman.

The little Jew looks him in the eye and says, "Sure, *now* it's a desert."

❖

Two goldfish are swimming around in a fish bowl. One goldfish asks the other, "Do you think there's a God?"

The second fish answers, "Of course there's a God."

To which the first fish says, "What makes you so certain there's a God?"

The second fish replies, "*Someone* changes the water."

❖

"My dear friend Moscowitz, this is your lucky day! Have I got a bargain for you! A big, healthy, Barnum & Bailey specially-trained elephant! And for you only, just a thousand dollars!"

"Are you crazy?!?" replies Moscowitz. "I live in a two-room apartment in a fourth floor walk-up. What do I want with an elephant? Why are you driving me crazy with 'I should buy an elephant'?"

"You're a tough man, Moscowitz. You drive a hard bargain. I'll tell you what I'm going to do. For another two hundred dollars, I'll throw in a beautiful baby elephant. Both elephants for only twelve hundred dollars!"

"Ah-ha! Now, now you're talking."

❖

Isaac is walking on the street in Tel Aviv when a stranger runs over to him and slaps him on the face. "That's for you, Moshe!" the stranger yells.

After recovering from the shock, Isaac starts to laugh.

"What are you laughing at?" the stranger asks. "Do you want me to hit you again?"

"No, please, no!" says Isaac, "It's just that the joke's on you—I'm not Moshe!"

❖

The rabbinical student is about to leave for America. When he asks his mentor for advice, the Rabbi offers an adage which he tells the student will guide him for the rest of his life. "Always remember," the Rabbi says sagely, "life is a fountain."

Deeply impressed by his teacher's wisdom, the student departs for a successful career in America. Thirty years later, he learns that the Rabbi is dying, so he returns for a final visit.

"Rabbi," he says, "I have one question. For 30 years, whenever I was was sad or confused, I thought about the phrase you passed on to me, and it has helped me through many difficult times. But to be perfectly frank, I have never understood the full meaning of it. Now that you are about to enter the Realm of Truth, tell me, dear Rabbi, why is life like a fountain?"

Wearily, the old man replied, "All right, so it's not like a fountain."

❖

Goldstein died of a heart attack two weeks after arriving in Florida for a vacation. His body is shipped back to New York, and two of Goldstein's friends come to see him in his casket.

One of them says, "Doesn't he look wonderful?"

"Yes," says the other. "Those two weeks in Florida did him a world of good!"

❖

Three Jews are condemned to death and stand before a firing squad. The officer asks the first man if he wants a blindfold. "Yes, sir, I do," he replies.

He asks the second man. "Yes, sir, I do, too," he replies.

He asks Sol, the third man. At the top of his voice, Sol shouts, "Absolutely not! This is an outrage! No blindfold! I want nothing from you despicable tyrants!"

The second man turns to him and in an anguished voice pleads, "Sol, please, don't make trouble!"

❖

A Texan visiting Israel asks a farmer about his farm.

"It's 35 meters in front and almost 50 meters out back. I raise a few chickens," the Israeli says with pride.

"I'm a farmer, too," says the Texan. "On my farm, I can drive from morning until sundown and not reach the end of my property."

"That's a shame," says the Israeli, shaking his head. "I once had a car like that."

❖

Rachel: "What's wrong with your hair, dear? It looks like a wig."

Ruth: "You know something—it is a wig!"

Rachel: "How do you like that! You could never tell."

❖

While visiting a cemetery, Moshe comes to a magnificent marble mausoleum. Chiseled above the doorway and inlaid in gold is the name **ROTHSCHILD**.

"Wow!" says Moshe. "That's what I call living!"

❖

Two brave firemen pull a drunken Izzy from the burning bed. They scream at him, "Izzy, you idiot! This will teach you not to smoke in bed."

"Who was smoking?" slurs Izzy. "This miserable bed was on fire when I got in!"

❖

Jennie: "What would you do if you found a million dollars?"

Sarah: "Well, if it was a poor person who lost it, I'd give it back!"

❖

Levi: "I heard you were turned down for the radio announcer's job."

Sidney: "You h-h-heard r-r-right. Wh-wh-who g-g-gives a Jew a ch-ch-chance?!?"

❖

Since all the seats at the posh synagogue were filled for the Yom Kippur service, the stranger was stopped at the door. "I just want to see Adam Rosenberg," the stranger pleaded. "I have an important message for him."

"OK, I'll let you talk to Rosenberg," said the usher suspiciously. "But I'll be watching, so don't let me catch you praying!"

❖

"Ladies and gentlemen," the stage manager announces, "I am terribly sorry to tell you that the great actor Moshe Strauss has had a fatal stroke in his dressing room, and we cannot continue tonight's performance."

A woman's voice from the second balcony cries out, "Quick, give him an enema!"

"Lady," says the manager, "the stroke was fatal."

"So give him an enema!" the woman shouts again.

"Strauss is dead. An enema can't possibly help."

The voice from the balcony: "Couldn't hurt."

❖

Max and Isaac come to the Rabbi's study to settle a dispute. The Rabbi's wife is also seated in the room.

Max explains his complaint to the Rabbi: the story is such and such, and he has to do this and he has to do that. He gives a fine account and argues his case clearly.

The Rabbi declares, "Max, you're right."

Next, Isaac presents his side. He speaks with such passion and persuasion that the Rabbi says to him, "Isaac, you're right."

After they leave, the Rabbi's wife is distraught and says to her husband, "They have conflicting stories. How can you say that both of them are right? When one wins, the other must lose."

The Rabbi thinks long and hard and finally says to his wife, "You know, you're right."

❖

Elderly Morris Rabinowitz is accidentally hit by a car while crossing Delancey Street. An ambulance is called and arrives quickly.

The emergency medical technician finds Morris laid out prone and bleeding on the sidewalk. He lifts the old man's head and asks solicitously, "Are you comfortable?"

Morris replies with pride, "I make a living."

❖

WHAT'S IN A NAME?

You know these Jewish comedy stars, but do you know the names they were born with? Try to match the well-known name on the left with the comic's name on his or her birth certificate on the right. (To start you off, Woody Allen was born Stewart Konisberg.)

Woody Allen	A. Jerome Silberman
Red Buttons	B. Milton Supman
Jerry Lewis	C. Irving Lahrheim
George Burns	D. Leonard Alfred Schneider
Judy Holiday	E. Isadore Itzkowitz
Buddy Hackett	F. Michael Igor Paschowsky
Joey Bishop	G. Joseph Gottleib
Jack Benny	H. Judith Tuvid
Mel Brooks	I. Jerome Levitch
Mike Nichols	J. David Kaminsky
Alan King	K. Stewart Konisberg
Shecky Green	L. Nathan Birnbaum
Danny Kaye	M. Leonard Hacker
Joey Adams	N. Benjamin Kubelsky
Lenny Bruce	O. Melvin Kaminsky
Eddie Cantor	P. Irwin Kniberg
Rodney Dangerfield	Q. Sheldon Greenfield
Burt Lahr	R. Joseph Abramowitz
Jackie Mason	S. Jacob Cohen
Joan Rivers	T. Yocov Maza
Soupy Sales	U. Joan Alexandra Molinsky
Gene Wilder	V. Richard Schulefand
Dick Shawn	W. Esaiah Edwin Leopold
Ed Wynn	X. Aaron Chwatt

The answers are on page 48.

**HOW TO
TELL A
JEWISH
JOKE**

T HE VETERAN JEWISH COMICS ARE SITTING at their usual
Stage Deli table, telling each other jokes. Since they know all
of the jokes anyway, they've developed a shorthand and given each
joke a number.

"Number 37!" says Bernie, and the group breaks up in laughter. Mannie counters with "53!" and again the table rocks with guffaws. Solly, the newcomer to the group, shouts, "44!"

Dead silence.

Solly turns to Manny and asks, "What's the matter? Isn't '44' a good joke?"

"Sure it's a good joke," Manny says. *"But the way you tell it..."*

***

There's an art to telling a joke well. If you've had the good
fortune to hear one of the masters—Buddy Hackett, Alan King, and
Mel Brooks come to mind—then you've heard the beautiful music of
a Jewish joke well told. But just as you need not be a virtuoso to
enjoy playing the piano, you don't have to be a master comedian to
enjoy telling a good joke.

Whether you're at a casual meal with a pal or a serious business meeting, telling a joke can establish contact, break the tension,
and create a friendly atmosphere for whatever comes next. A good

joke delivered with panache is money in the bank. But, like any worthwhile skill, the ability to tell a joke well must be honed to get the desired results.

Jokes, of course, are everywhere, from TV comics to the Internet to a monthly page in *Playboy*. For reliable material, however, memorize and practice telling some of the jokes in this book. They are well-aged and have withstood the test of time.

As you practice, keep these tips in mind...

○ Is the joke appropriate for this time, place, and audience? If not, just tell it in your mind and chuckle to yourself.

○ There are two parts to most jokes: the set-up and the punch line. The sure way to kill a joke is with a long, windy set-up. According to humorist Larry Wilde, "The size of the laugh you get is inversely proportionate to the number of words used to reach the punch line. The fewer the words, the bigger the laughs." A good joke illustrates this point: As he reached the end of a long, drawn-out story, the convention speaker realized he was losing his audience and said, "To make a long story short..." A voice from the back of the room called out, "It's too late now!"

○ During the set-up, avoid surplus detail. Does it matter whether the fly was in chicken soup or barley soup? Does it matter whether it happened in a restaurant in Peoria or in Milwaukee? No? Then leave it out.

○ For a joke to work, the punch line must be a surprise, so be careful not to give it away! If your audience guesses the punch line before you've finished the joke, you've lost the surprise. Just as a magician distracts you until a rabbit rises from the hat, a good joke-teller must lead the audience in another direction until the punch line ("Take my wife—*please!*"). The punch line is the most important part of any joke. Memorize it *exactly* so you can repeat it without stumbling.

○ Make sure you have the story straight in your mind before you start the joke. Many a good joke died on arrival because the teller garbled the set-up or omitted The Crucial Fact: "Oh, I forgot to tell you, this was his *third* wife..."

○ Try to find a natural transition into your joke, and don't hesitate to create your own version of a joke. Add personal touches and details appropriate to the moment, or change the locale to a place familiar to your audience. Also, you'll add to the humor if there's a semblance of truth to the story.

○ Does the humor in your story come from the surprise of the entire last sentence or from the emphasis on just a word or two? Either way, it's the punch line, so punch it out smartly.

○ I'm often amazed when I hear roars of laughter at a joke that's been around a long time. Remember: there are no new jokes, only new audiences. So don't be afraid to bring out a "golden oldie" one more time. (Worst case scenario: they've heard it before. If so, you can make a partial recovery by saying, "I wasn't trying to tell you a new joke—I was trying to refresh your memory.")

○ Don't explain your gag after you've told it. If it needs explaining, you shouldn't tell it.

○ It takes a sharp ear and verbal skill to tell a story in dialect. If you try and fail, they'll be laughing *at* you instead of *with* you. So unless you're really good at it, don't use dialect. If it's a good joke, it will stand up in plain English.

○ Have the courage to fail. If your joke dies, let it die with dignity. Shrug it off or learn from it. Even the pros tell stinkers now and then. Johnny Carson got his biggest laughs from the self-deprecating wisecracks he told after a joke failed.

○ There is as much—and probably more—pleasure in telling a funny story than there is in hearing it. So, enjoy the story yourself. Your delivery should reflect your pleasure.

○ Listen to the way a pro tells jokes. With practice, you can imitate the timing, the inflection, and the body language to get the big laughs.

○ You get better at telling a joke the same way you get to Carnegie Hall—practice, practice, practice!

A final word about listening to someone else tell a joke:

A person of breeding and character has never heard the joke before. Revealing the punch line while the joke is being told is punishable by death. No matter how often you've heard it before, how unfunny the joke may be, or how badly it is told, be nice. Act amused and reward the storyteller with, at the very least, a chuckle and a smile. The better you get at this, the more friends you'll have.

Here are the answers to What's in a Name. How many did you get?

Woody Allen = K, Stewart Konisberg
Red Buttons = X, Aaron Chwatt
Jerry Lewis = I, Jerome Levitch
George Burns = L, Nathan Birnbaum
Judy Holiday = H, Judith Tuvid
Buddy Hackett = M, Leonard Hacker
Joey Bishop = G, Joseph Gottleib
Jack Benny = N, Benjamin Kubelsky
Mel Brooks = O, Melvin Kaminsky
Mike Nichols = F, Michael Igor Paschowsky
Alan King = P, Irwin Kniberg
Shecky Green = Q, Sheldon Greenfield
Danny Kaye = J, David Kaminsky
Joey Adams = R, Joseph Abramowitz
Lenny Bruce = D, Leonard Alfred Schneider
Eddie Cantor = E, Isadore Itzkowitz
Rodney Dangerfield = S, Jacob Cohen
Burt Lahr = C, Irving Lahrheim
Jackie Mason = T, Yocov Maza
Joan Rivers = U, Joan Alexandra Molinsky
Soupy Sales = B, Milton Supman
Gene Wilder = A, Jerome Silberman
Dick Shawn = V, Richard Schulefand
Ed Wynn = W, Esaiah Edwin Leopold

Food

Millie: "The food here is terrible."
Ruth: "Yes, and such small portions!"

A Jewish gentleman stood before a delicatessen display counter and pointed to a tray. "I'll have a pound of that salmon," he said.

"That's not salmon," the clerk said. "It's ham."

"Mister," the customer snapped, "in case nobody ever told you, you got a big mouth!"

❖

Goldberg was the neighborhood smart aleck. When he saw the sign in the deli that said *We Serve Every Type of Sandwich*, he called the waiter over.

"Is that sign true?" Goldberg asked.

"Absolutely, positively! We serve every type of sandwich," the waiter replied proudly.

"Then bring me an elephant sandwich on toast," Goldberg said.

A slight pause and the waiter replied, "I'm sorry, Mr. Goldberg, but for just one sandwich, we can't start another elephant."

❖

A man from Mars lands on Second Avenue in the lower East Side of New York. He goes into a Jewish bakery and asks, "What are those little wheels in the window?"

"Those aren't wheels," says the storekeeper. "They're called bagels. Here, try one..."

The Martian bites into the bagel and says, "Hey! This would go great with some lox and cream cheese!"

❖

Jack Grossman, a garment salesman on the road, stopped his car on the main street of a small town in rural Alabama. Tired and hungry and unable to find a restaurant, he walked into a general store that sold hardware and farm supplies and also served food.

"What can I do for you?" the proprietor asked.

"You handle maybe fertilizer?"

"Sure do!"

"Good," said Grossman. "Wash your hands and make me a cheese sandwich."

❖

Sol and Herbie were finishing their lunch in a New York restaurant when the waiter asked, "Tea or coffee, gentlemen?"

"I'll have tea," said Sol.

"Me too," said Herbie. "And make sure the glass is clean."

The waiter returned in a few minutes and announced, "Two teas! And which one gets the clean glass?"

❖

Benjy finally found a birthday gift for his mother: a parrot that spoke Yiddish. When he called her to find out how she liked the present, she said, "Delicious!"

"Mama, you ate a parrot that speaks Yiddish?!?" he cried.

"So," she said, "if he could talk, why didn't he say something?"

❖

Assimilation

"Only in America!"

Cohen and Goldberg were partners in the dress business, and business was terrible. Cohen decided to change his name—and maybe change his luck. From now on, he would be O'Brien. Goldberg thought Cohen had a good idea and announced that he, too, would change his name to O'Brien.

The next day, a caller to the firm of O'Brien & O'Brien asked to speak to Mr. O'Brien immediately.

"Which O'Brien?" the operator asked. "Cohen or Goldberg?"

❖

Mrs. Ginzberg stops at Rosemarie de Paris, an elegant Fifth Avenue patisserie, and says, "Please, can you gimme two pounds of those chocolates?"

The haughty clerk replies, "Madam means the bonbons, no doubt."

"Okay," Mrs. Ginzberg says. "Also, some of them fancy cookies."

"Ah, you mean our *petits fours*," the clerk says. "Shall we deliver these in our Rolls-Royce limousine?"

"Nah," says Mrs. Ginzberg. "I'll take 'em with me."

This was too much for the clerk. "Madam," he says proudly, "from Rosemarie de Paris you don't *shlep!*"

❖

Epstein is eating in a Chinese restaurant. To his surprise, he discovers while ordering his meal that the Chinese waiter is speaking fluent Yiddish.

When Epstein pays the check, he compliments the owner. "How did you manage that even the Chinese waiter speaks Yiddish?"

The owner replies in a whisper, "Shhhhh! Not so loud. He thinks we're teaching him English."

❖

Mrs. Shapiro was walking along Delancey Street and stopped at a dry goods store with the sign Rabinowitz & O'Brien. She decided to compliment the man behind the counter—a small, dark-haired man with a beard and a yarmulke.

"It's nice to see how the Jews and the Irish have become such good friends and have even become business partners. My compliments!" said Mrs. Shapiro.

"I've got more news for you, lady," the man said. "I'm O'Brien."

❖

After many years, a young Talmud student who had left the old country for America returns to visit the family.

"But—where is your beard?" asks his mother upon seeing him.

"Mama," he replies, "in America, nobody wears a beard."

"But at least you keep the Sabbath?"

"Mama, business is business. In America, everybody works on the Sabbath."

"But kosher food you still eat?"

"Mama, in America, it is very difficult to keep kosher."

The old lady ponders this information and then leans over and whispers in his ear, "Isaac, tell me—you're still circumcised?"

❖

Benny Lipshitz struck it rich and bought himself a large, fully appointed yacht. After all, the rich and powerful owned yachts. Dressed in an impressive-looking captain's outfit, he showed the

yacht to his elderly mother and father visiting from the Bronx.

"Mama," he asked, "what do you think of your son, the Captain?"

"Listen, Benny, darling," his mother replied. "By Papa, you're a Captain. By me, you're a Captain. By you, you're a Captain. But, believe me, by a Captain, you're no Captain!"

❖

Desperate to enter the high-society, country club scene, Abe and Sarah Finkelstein changed their names to Tyrone and Courtney Farnsworth. At the party welcoming them into the Briar Ridge Country Club, they were seated with the Fillmores, the Hamptons, and the Wilsons. As he was serving dinner, the gloved waiter in white tie and tails tripped and dumped an entire bowl of hot soup in Courtney Farnsworth's lap.

"*Oy veh!*" yelled Courtney—but swiftly added, "Whatever *that* means!"

❖

When he went into show business, Sheldon Cohen changed his name to William Montgomery. To celebrate his starring performance on Broadway, he gave a grand party at his penthouse apartment in the high-rent district. He asked his mother to come to the party, but she never arrived.

The next morning he found his mother sitting quietly in the lobby of building. He asked her what she was doing there and why she didn't come to party.

"I couldn't find your apartment," she said.

"Why didn't you ask the doorman?" he asked.

"I wanted to," she replied, "but to tell you the truth, I forgot your name."

❖

Doctors

*"Jews believe that a fetus is a fetus
until it gets out of medical school."*

*"If you want to drive a doctor crazy, the next time
he tells you to strip to the waist, take off your pants."*

Ninety-year-old Sam Bialostock explained his problem to his psychiatrist: "Three months ago, I met a beautiful 26-year-old woman. I took her home, and she moved in with me. Every day she makes love to me in the morning, after lunch, and then again at night."

"For a 90-year-old man, that's great!" said the analyst. "What's your problem?"

Sam sighed, "I can't remember where I live."

❖

A man walks into a psychiatrist's office and says, "Doc, I'm going crazy. I keep imagining I'm a zebra. I look at myself in the mirror, and I see my entire body covered with black stripes."

The doctor says, "You are not a zebra. Calm down, go home, take these pills, and get a good night's sleep. I'm sure the black stripes will disappear."

The man goes home and takes the pills. Next day, he's back.

"Doc," he says, "the black stripes disappeared! I feel great! Now, got anything for the white stripes?"

❖

A troubled senior citizen confided in his psychiatrist, "Doc, I'm very worried about my future. What's going to happen to me? Can you help me with all this anxiety I feel?"

"Yes, I can help," the psychiatrist replied. "You must see me twice a week for a year at $100 per visit. And I must have the money in advance."

"Okay, Doc," the man says. "And now that your future is assured, how about mine?"

❖

Esther is complaining to the psychiatrist about her husband: "It's terrible," she says. "He thinks he's a racehorse. He wants to live in a stable, he walks on all fours, and he even eats hay. Please tell me, doctor, can you cure him?"

"I'm sure that I can," the analyst responds, "but I have to be honest with you—the treatment will be long and expensive."

"Oh, money's no object," Esther replied. "He's already won two races."

❖

Two psychiatrists are leaving work together after a long day.

"Dr. Plotkin, I don't know how you do it," the younger psychiatrist says. "My patients are driving me crazy. All day long they come in with their complaints, their problems, and their troubles. Don't you get tired and depressed having to sit there day after day and listen to them?"

"Ah ha," replies Plotkin. "Who listens?"

❖

Guy walks down the street yelling, "Call me a doctor! Call me a doctor! Call me a doctor!..."

A passerby asks, "What's the matter? Are you sick?"

He says, "No, I just graduated from medical school!"

❖

Dr. Klein had bad news for his 83-year-old patient: "Mrs. Adler, because we've been friends for so long I'm going to tell you something I don't usually tell a patient. I'm sorry, but you are going to die. Is there someone you'd like to see?"

"Yes," the old lady answered. "I'd like to see another doctor!"

❖

When the Park Avenue doctor's snooty receptionist told Milton Blum that his visit would cost $75, he said, "I don't have it."

"You don't have it—and you have the nerve to come to the country's leading specialist, an expensive Park Avenue doctor?" she said haughtily.

Rising in righteous indignation, Blum exclaimed, "Madam, when it comes to my health, money is no object!"

❖

Man goes to a psychiatrist and complains, "No one listens to me. No one talks to me."

Doctor says, "Next!"

❖

"You're in great shape," the doctor says. "You'll live to be 70."

"But, doctor, I'm 72," says the patient.

"*Nu*?" the doctor replies. "Did I lie?"

❖

Doctor: "The check you gave me came back!"

Shlomele: "So did my arthritis!"

❖

A faith healer asked Moshe how his family was getting along. "They're all fine," Moshe said, "except my uncle. He's very sick."

"Your uncle is not sick," the faith healer said. "He *thinks* he's sick."

Two weeks later, the faith healer ran into Moshe on the street. "How is your uncle getting along?" he asked.

Moshe shrugged, "He *thinks* he's dead."

❖

At her daughter's urging, Mrs. Goldberg, age 75, went to see a gynecologist for the first time in her life. She answered the nurse's questions and then was asked to step behind a screen and remove her clothes so Dr. Kaplan could examine her.

At some point during the examination, Mrs. Goldberg said, "Excuse me, Doctor. Can I ask a you question?"

"Certainly," the doctor replied.

"Tell me," she said. "Your mother knows that from this you make a living?"

❖

Kittzleman gets a call from his doctor with the results of his blood test. "I've got bad news and worse news," says the doctor. "The bad news is, you've only got 24 hours to live."

"Oh, no," says Kittzleman. "That's terrible. How could it possibly get worse than that?"

"I've been trying to reach you since yesterday."

❖

A Brief Guide to

COMMON YIDDISH TERMS

**"He's billing us for answering a question
on the phone? That's *chutzpa*!"**

**"I want to make sure everything's *kosher*
before we go ahead with the deal."**

THOSE TWO WORDS—*CHUTZPA* AND *KOSHER*—can come in quite handy no matter what your religion.

Chutzpa means unmitigated nerve or gall. A man goes bankrupt, takes a cab to the creditors' meeting, and invites the cab driver in as one of the creditors—that's *chutzpa*! He kills his mother and father and pleads for mercy on the grounds that he's an orphan—that's *chutzpa*! You get the idea.

The original meaning of *kosher* is "fit to eat" and ritually clean in accordance with *kashrut*, the Jewish dietary laws. In American slang, kosher means legitimate, proper, the real thing, on the up and up, etc.

Like bagels and lox, many Yiddish words and Jewish terms have become part of the general culture. A few of these rich, pungent words dropped at the right moment or used properly in a Jewish joke will enhance your vocabulary and your joke-telling style.

Bar Mitzvah—the ceremony at which a 13-year-old Jewish boy announces, "Today I am a man." And he is. With the adult status comes the obligation to live a religious, ethical life. The ceremony for girls is called *bas* (or *bat*) *mitzvah*.

Borsht—beet soup. Hot or cold, it's delicious, especially with small boiled potatoes and a dab of sour cream on top. It was the favorite dish of Jews who lived around New York City and vacationed in the Catskill Mountains (hence the term, the "Borsht Belt").

Chanukah—also, *Hanukkah*. This eight-day celebration, usually in December, commemorates a Jewish victory over Syrian despots in 167 BC and is observed with parties, special food, gifts to children, and the lighting of a special candelabrum called a *menorah*.

Kibitz—(The accent is on the first syllable.) When a spectator makes unsolicited comments during a card game or other proceeding, he's just there to *kibitz*. ("Don't let him bluff you—stay and raise him! Oh, well...")

Kvell—to swell with pride and pleasure. Usually used to describe a Jewish parent's reaction to a child or grandchild.

L'chayim—a toast that means, "To life!" Equivalent to *skoal, salud, prosit,* etc.

Luftmensch—an impractical fellow, someone with his head in the clouds and a million ideas that never work. The character Kramer on *Seinfeld* is a perfect example.

Maven—an expert, a specialist, a connoisseur, a knowledgeable judge of quality. ("Before we buy that equipment, we'll need to talk to a computer *maven*.")

Megillah—a long, boring rigmarole or a tedious, complicated matter. In a historic debate, Abraham Lincoln gave a speech that was short and sweet, while his opponent, Stephen Douglas, delivered the whole *megillah*. You know who won.

Mazel—good luck. The common Jewish phrase for congratulations and luck is *"mazel tov!"* According to humorist Sam Levenson, *mazel* is something only your competitor has.

Mensch—an upright, trustworthy person, worthy of respect. According to Leo Rosten, neither wealth nor status nor success qualifies one to be called a *mensch*. You've got to earn it by your behavior and reputation.

Nosh—a snack, a tasty bite usually eaten between meals. If you're at a cocktail party and you're offered something with a toothpick in it—go ahead, *nosh*.

Nu?—Always followed by a question mark, it means "So?" The plaintive shrug that goes with it is silent.

Shadchen—a professional matchmaker. Hello, Dolly!

A *shleimazl* is a born loser; everything bad happens to him. A *shlemiel* can't do anything right. (The *shlemiel* waiter drops a plate of hot soup; it lands in the *shleimazl's* lap.) In comedy, the Three Stooges were classic *shlemiels*, while Rodney Dangerfield and Woody Allen define *shleimazls*.

Shlep—As a verb, *shlep* means to pull, carry, or drag, or to move slowly and awkwardly. As a noun, the word can mean a tedious journey or connote a bum, a loser, a drag on society: "You know that blind date I had? I'll never see him again. He was a real *shlep!*"

Shmaltz—This Yiddish word for chicken fat is now used to describe exaggerated sentimentality, especially in music, literature, and film (e.g., *Love Story* and *The Bridges of Madison County*). *Shmaltzy* is the wonderful adjective.

Shnoz—It just means a nose, but *shnoz* is usually reserved for unusually large examples. Groucho Marx, Barbra Streisand, and Jimmy Durante are entertainers famous for their shnozzes.

Shtick—Usually used to describe a performer's attention-stealing actions, it can also describe any characteristic gesture or entertaining gimmick: George Burns' cigar, Groucho Marx's wiggling eyebrows and duck-walk, etc.

Tummler—Literally, it means a person who creates a commotion, but at a resort hotel in the Catskills, it's a job description. To keep guests amused and diverted between meals, the hotel *tummler* conducts morning callisthenics, clowns around the pool in the afternoon, and tells jokes and stages skits in the evening. Jerry Lewis, Mel Brooks, Milton Berle, and just about every great U.S. Jewish comedy star began their careers as *tummlers*.

Business

"Irving accumulated millions making men's suits.
He lost it all making one skirt."

"There's a secret method for making a small fortune
in Las Vegas: Start with a large fortune."

"The garment business is so bad," Sam Glickman kvetched. "The last two years, I've been losing $3,000 a week."

"Then why don't you give up the business?" his friend asked.

"So how am I going to make a living?"

❖

Silverstein went into a small grocery store and asked, "Do you have any salt?"

"Hoo-boy, do we have salt! Come, look back here," said the owner as he took Silverstein into the back room, which contained nothing but salt—19 barrels of salt.

"Wow!" Silverstein said. "You really must know how to sell salt."

"Not me," said the owner. "I'm not so good at it. But the salesman I bought it from—*he can sell salt!*"

❖

Mr. Weiss ordered a pair of pants from a local tailor. When they were not ready in the promised two weeks, Weiss agreed to wait another two weeks…and then another two weeks…until finally, after six months, the tailor presented him with his new pants and displayed them proudly for everyone to see.

"I want to ask you a question," Weiss said to the tailor. "How come God Almighty was able to create the world—the entire universe!—in only six days, and it took you *six months* to make a pair of pants?"

"Ah," replied the tailor. "Look at the condition of the world—and look at this gorgeous pair of pants!"

❖

A young man brought his pants to a tailor to have them altered. The next day, he was called to London on a last-minute job assignment.

He returned home five years later. While dressing, he reached into his jacket pocket and found the tailor's receipt for his pants. He went to the tailor's shop, handed him the receipt, and asked, "Are my pants here?"

"Yes," said the tailor. "Be ready next Tuesday."

❖

The Pharaoh decided to go for a ride up the Nile.

"Get 80 Jewish slaves for oarsmen," he commanded.

Murray was among the Jews in chains in the hold, all of them rowing at a furious pace. As the trip ended, Murray turned to Ben sitting next to him and asked, "Tell me, Ben. On a cruise like this, how much do you tip the whipper?"

❖

A marriage broker offered Morty a beautiful young girl, a real prize, to be his wife. But Morty was stubborn.

"I'm a businessman," Morty argued. "Before I buy material from a mill, I look at swatches. So before I get married, I gotta have a sample also."

The broker had no choice but to relay the message to the girl. "He says he's a good businessman, and he has to know exactly what he's buying. He insists on a sample."

"Listen," the girl replied, "I'm also good at business. A sample I don't give. But I will give him references!"

❖

Even though he was in his late 70's, Simmelweiss, the neighborhood painter, accepted an odd job every so often. He was relaxing at home after painting a Park Avenue apartment when the lady of the house called and asked him to come back right away.
It seems that the night before, the woman's husband had accidentally smeared the wet paint in the bedroom.

So when Simmelweiss showed up at the door, the woman said, "Oh, I'm so glad you could come back today. Come into the bedroom with me—I want to show you where my husband put his hand last night."

"Listen, lady," Simmelweiss sighed, "I'm not so young anymore. Just give me a glass of tea with lemon. *That* I'll appreciate."

❖

God & Religion

"God, I know we are the chosen people, but couldn't you choose somebody else for a change?"—Sholom Aleichem

*"I know the Lord will help us.
But help us, Lord, before you help us."*

A poor Jew walking in the forest feels close enough to God to ask, "God, what is a million years to you?"

God replies, "My son, a million years to you is like a second to me."

The man asks, "God, what is a million dollars to you?"

God replies, "My son, a million dollars to you is less than a penny to me. It means almost nothing to me."

The man asks, "So God, can I have a million dollars?"

And God replies, "In a second."

❖·

Grandma Esther was walking along the beach with her cherished five-year-old grandson by her side. Suddenly, a huge wave washed over them and swept the child out to sea.

"Oh, Lord!" cried the grandmother. "What have you done? That boy is my whole life! If you'll just bring that boy back alive, I'll do anything. I'll be the best person. I'll give to charity. I'll work for the poor and the sick. I'll go to the synagogue every day. Please, God, please, just give me back my boy!"

At that moment, another huge wave came up and washed the child onto the sand, safe and sound. His grandmother looked at the boy, then looked up to heaven.

"Okay," she said. "So where's his hat?"

❖

Seymour Kittleman was a good and pious man, and when he passed away the Lord Himself greeted him at the pearly gates of heaven.

"Hungry, Seymour?" the Lord asked.

"I could eat," said Kittleman. The Lord opened a can of tuna, and they shared it.

While eating his humble meal, Kittleman looked down into Hell and noticed the inhabitants devouring enormous steaks, pheasant, pastries, and vodka.

The next day, the Lord again asked Kittleman if he were hungry, and Kittleman again said, "I could eat." Once again, a can of tuna was opened and shared, while down below Kittleman noticed a feast of caviar, champagne, lamb, truffles, brandy, and chocolates.

The following day, mealtime arrived and another can of tuna was opened. Meekly, Kittleman said, "Lord, I am very happy to be in heaven as a reward for the good life I lived. But, this *is* heaven, and all I get to eat is tuna. But in the Other Place, they eat like kings. I just don't understand."

"To be honest, Seymour," the Lord said, "for just two people, does it pay to cook?"

❖

Two men sitting on a train are talking. One guy says, "Did you hear the one about the two Jews who are walking down the street…"

Other guy says, "Hold it! Why are you always telling jokes about Jews? I find it offensive. Why must they always be about Jews?"

"You're right," his friend replies and starts the joke again: "So, these two Chinamen are walking down the street on the way to their nephew's bar mitzvah…"

❖

After many years shipwrecked on a desert island, Kaplan is rescued by a passing ship. Before leaving for home, he shows the ship's Captain around the island. He points out the house he built from twigs and rocks and the vegetable garden he built to provide food. He then takes the Captain to the water's edge and shows him the lovely synagogue he built.

"If this is the synagogue, then what's that building over there?" the Captain asks.

Kaplan explains, "This is the synagogue that I go to. And that— that's the synagogue I *don't* go to."

❖

When Bernie's wife died after a long illness, Bernie decided that he would take a new lease on life. He went to a spa, lost 30 pounds, had plastic surgery, and bought himself an expensive toupee. As he was leaving an exclusive men's store in his new Armani suit, he was hit

by a truck and killed on the spot.

In heaven, Bernie asked his Maker, "God, why me? I was a good husband, a religious man. I gave to charity. Why now, when after all these years I have a chance to live a little, why do you let this happen to me?"

The Lord replied, "To tell you the truth, Bernie, I just didn't recognize you!"

❖

Father Flaherty is sitting in the confessional booth when he hears an unfamiliar voice with a heavy Jewish accent.

"Father, my name is Morris Lipsky. I am 79 years old. I am currently involved with a 24-year-old girl and also, on the side, with her 19-year-old sister. We engage in all manner of sexual pleasure, and in my whole life I never felt better!"

"My good man," asks the priest, "are you a Catholic?"

Lipsky replied, "No, father, I'm not."

"Then why are you telling me?"

Lipsky replied proudly, "I'm telling everybody!"

❖

The young rabbi was an avid golfer. Even on Yom Kippur, the holiest day of the year, a day for fasting and atonement, he snuck out to play nine holes by himself.

On the seventh hole, he teed off and a gust of wind carried the ball

directly from the tee into the cup. A hole in one!

An angel observing this miracle addressed God angrily, "Lord, the rabbi is playing golf on Yom Kippur, you cause the wind to give him a hole in one—and you call this a punishment?"

God smiled. "Sure it is," He said. "Who can he tell?"

❖

Judges, Matchmakers, & Other Characters

*"A man jumps from the tallest building in the city,
and as he passes the 40th floor he thinks,
'So far, not bad at all.'"*

80-year-old Bessie Feingold bursts into the rec room of the men's retirement home. She holds her clenched fist in the air and announces, "Anyone who can guess what's in my hand can have sex with me tonight!"

An elderly gentlemen in the rear shouts out, "An elephant?"

Bessie thinks a minute and declares, "Close enough!"

❖

Every night after the performance, women lined up at the stage door to greet the great Yiddish stage star Boris Thomashefsky.

One night, he took a voluptuous young female fan to bed. The next morning, he presented her with two orchestra tickets for that evening's show.

"Oh, Mr. Thomashefsky," she cried. "Thank you, but I am poor. Tickets I don't need. I need bread."

"Bread!" he boomed. "Thomashefsky gives tickets. You want bread, go sleep with a baker!"

❖

"How was your golf game, Sam?"

"The course was beautiful, it was a lovely day, and I was playing a great game. But then, on the fifth hole, my partner Cohen drops dead! After that it was terrible—hit the ball, shlep Cohen...hit the ball, shlep Cohen...hit the ball, shlep Cohen..."

❖

Ginsburg, shabbily dressed and bowed with age, goes up to the receptionist at a large corporate headquarters and demands to see the personnel director—no one else will do.

When the personnel director appears, Ginsburg asks, "Did you advertise in the *New York Times* for an MBA with a postgraduate degree in analytical mathematics and extensive experience in statistical analysis and multinational monetary negotiation?"

"Yes, we did," replies the personnel director.

"Well then," says Ginsburg, "I want you should know, on me you can't count."

❖

A matchmaker, singing the praises of a female client, brings an eligible young man to see her. He takes one look at the woman and turns away to whisper to the matchmaker, "You said she was young, and she's 50 for sure. You said she was beautiful, and she's ugly as sin. You said she was shapely, and she's big enough for two, you said..."

"You don't have to whisper," says the matchmaker. "She's also hard of hearing."

❖

Teitelbaum, nervous and sick on his first airplane ride, threw up on the expensive gown of the lady asleep in the next seat. When she awoke, she was in shock at the mess all over her.

Teitelbaum leans over and asks, "You feel better now?"

❖

A drunken heckler to a stand-up comic: "You are the ugliest man I've ever seen!"

The comic replies, "You're drunk."

"Yeah," says the heckler, "but *I'll* be sober in the morning!"

❖

The courtroom was silent while the judge pondered the papers in the paternity suit before him. As he turned over the last document, he reached into his robe, drew out a cigar, and handed it to the defendant.

"Congratulations, Mr. Bernstein!" he boomed. "You've just become a father!"

❖

Mrs. Rothstein telephoned the president of Neiman Marcus at 4:00 a.m. and said, "I just want to tell you how much I like the hat I bought."

"That's very nice, madam," said the department store executive. "But why did you wake me up at four in the morning just to tell me that?"

"Because," said Mrs. Rothstein, "they just delivered it!"

❖

The phone rang at the law offices of Goldstein, Goldstein & Goldstein: "Hello, may I please speak with Mr. Goldstein?"

"Mr. Goldstein is in court."

"Well then, can I speak to Mr. Goldstein?"

"Sorry, he's on vacation."

"Okay, then I'll speak to Mr. Goldstein."

"Speaking."

❖

Rebecca Solwitz decided to vacation in Hawaii. When she arrived at the Honolulu airport, she approached a clerk.

"You look like a native," she said. "What is the correct way to pronounce the name of your state? Is it Ha*w*aii or Ha*v*aii?"

"Ha*v*aii," the man answered.

"Thank you," she said.

"You're *v*elcome!" he replied.

❖

A matchmaker brings her assistant with her to offer a bride to the town's most eligible bachelor. Her assistant comes along to confirm the matchmaker's description of the proposed bride.

"She is as straight as a pine tree," the matchmaker says.

"As a pine tree!" the assistant echoes.

"And she has beautiful eyes," the matchmaker continues.

"What eyes she has!" the assistant affirms.

"It's true there is one thing," admits the matchmaker. "She has a small hump."

And the assistant's confirmation rings out, "And what a hump!"

❖

A rabbi gets caught in a downpour and ducks into a Chinese restaurant. Fully soused after many drinks, he leans over the bar and punches the bartender. "That's for Pearl Harbor!" he says.

"Are you crazy?!?" asks the bartender. "Pearl Harbor was the Japanese. I'm Chinese."

"So? Japanese, Chinese—what's the difference?" the rabbi says. "Here, lemme buy you a drink."

After a few drinks, the bartender leans over the bar and knocks the rabbi off his seat.

"What was that for?!?" the rabbi cries.

"That was for the Titanic," the bartender says.

"The Titanic?!?" the rabbi says. "That was sunk by an iceberg!"

"So?" says the bartender. "Iceberg, Goldberg—what's the difference?"

❖

An elderly man is sitting on a park bench reading a newspaper. A bird flies overhead and a copious dropping lands on the man's best navy blue suit.

He looks up, shakes his first in fury, and cries out, "For others, you sing!"

❖

Cohen, a menswear manufacturer, returns from a two-week vacation in Italy.

"So, how was the trip?" his partner asks.

"Great, wonderful," Cohen replies.

"Did you get to see the Pope?"

"Of course."

"So?"

"Seems to me, a 39 short."

❖

At age 79, Leo announces that he's marrying a 22-year-old girl.

"Are you crazy?!?" his friend says. "Don't you realize that at your age, sex with a young woman could be dangerous—even fatal!"

"Well," replies Leo, "if she dies, she dies."

❖

While Pinsky was on vacation, his brother was taking care of his beloved cat. When Pinsky returned, his brother announced, "Your cat is dead."

Pinsky was inconsolable. He said to his brother, "To tell me in such a way that my cat had passed on was cruel. You should have broken the news to me more gently. First, you could have said that my cat was playing on the roof. Later, you could have told me that he fell off. The next day you could have said that he broke a leg and that the vet had to operate. Then, when I came to pick him up, you could have said that he passed away during the night."

"I'm sorry," his brother replied. "I'll know better next time."

"Now tell me," Pinsky said, "how is Mama?"

The brother said, "Well, she was playing on the roof..."

❖

IT'␨ YOUR TURN!

Yes, we know—your favorite Jewish joke is not in the book. Or, despite our claim that there are no new Jewish jokes, you've just heard a one that's destined to be a classic. In either case, be a *mensch* and send it to us. You'll have the satisfaction of knowing that you helped create a gem or added to the inventory of classics.

Here's the deal: share your Jewish joke with us and, if we use it, you'll receive our gratitude, recognition in *Classic Jewish Jokes* II, and a free, autographed copy of the sequel. Write to

Robert Menchin
Jewish Jokes Archives
Mustang Publishing
P.O. Box 770426
Memphis, TN 38177 • USA

They're the Top!

From the Yiddish stage to burlesque, vaudeville, and Broadway, from humble beginnings in a Borscht-belt comedy mill to radio, TV, and films, through the dark years of the Holocaust to the happy years of freedom and opportunity in the American melting pot, these Jewish-American masters of comedy have made us laugh.

The following is a brief tribute to my five favorite Jewish comedy acts: Woody Allen, Henny Youngman, Rodney Dangerfield, The Marx Brothers, and Jerry Seinfeld.

WOODY ALLEN

Despite recent controversy in his love life, Woody Allen remains one of the great comic talents of the late 20th century. In his teens, he wrote routines for Sid Caesar, Buddy Hackett, Jack Paar, and other TV personalities. Shy and nervous, he failed as a stand-up comic but went on to create many classic films, such as **Take the Money and Run, Broadway Danny Rose, Zelig,** and **Annie Hall** (which won Academy Awards for writing and direction).

Woody portrays—and is!—a neurotic city-dweller struggling against the anxieties of a cold, mechanized world. In one of his fantasies, an armed squad from the local library surrounds his house to retrieve an overdue book. His comic effect is often achieved by juxtaposing the profound and the mundane, as when he describes his parents' values as "God and carpeting." In his writing, Allen finds humor in a shleimiel's confessions:

Abused: "I once won two weeks at an interfaith camp, where I was sadistically beaten by kids of all races and colors."

Insecure: "I used to steal second base and felt guilty and went back."

Intellectual: "In college I took courses called Truth, Beauty, and Advanced Truth and Beauty. I was expelled for cheating on the metaphysics exam; I looked into the soul of the boy sitting next to me."

Practical: "Bisexuality instantly doubles your chances for a date Saturday night."

HENNY YOUNGMAN

With his compact phrasing, rapid-fire delivery, and quick transition from topic to topic, Henny Youngman has earned the title "King of the One-Liners." His most famous line, "Take my wife—please!" typifies his style of humor. Considered a comic's comic, his classic lines would fill an entire book, but here are a few:

"A fellow walked up to me and said, 'Do you see a cop around here?' I said, 'No.' He said, 'Stick 'em up!'"

"I was so ugly when I was born that the doctor slapped my mother."

"Last night I baited a mousetrap with a picture of cheese. I caught a picture of a mouse."

"I haven't spoken to my wife in three weeks. I didn't want to interrupt her."

RODNEY DANGERFIELD

A mass of twitching, bug-eyed neurosis, Rodney Dangerfield was born Jacob Cohen in Babylon, New York. After an up-and-down career, he became rich and famous by lamenting his insecurity in nightclubs, TV specials, and hit films like **Back to School** and **Caddyshack**. Most of Rodney's humor is an extension of his immortal tag line, "I don't get no respect!"

"I tell ya, I don't get no respect. My kid goes to a private school. He won't tell me where."

"Yesterday I called to get the correct time. The recording hung up on me!"

"No respect at all. My mother never breastfed me. She told me she liked me as a friend."

"I went to a pharmacy to buy some rat poison. The clerk asks me, 'Should I wrap that up or are you going to eat it here?' I tell ya, I don't get no respect!"

THE MARX BROTHERS

Perhaps only Charlie Chaplin can match the comedy accomplishments of the deliciously zany Marx brothers: Groucho (Julius), Harpo (Adolph), and Chico (Leonard). In their classic films—**Animal Crackers, Duck Soup, A Day at the Races,** and many more—the multi-talented brothers poked fun at class distinction, punctured pomposity, and staged their unique assault on high culture. Chico, with his fake Italian accent, Harpo, the master of articulate silence, and Groucho, the snide court jester, created art from comic chaos.

Groucho's cutting wit is legendary. On his TV show **You Bet Your Life**, he interviewed a woman who had given birth to 22 children. "I love my husband," she explained. *"I love my cigar, too,"* Groucho replied, *"but I take it out of my mouth once in a while."*

Another time, Groucho wrote to the Friar's Club: *"Please accept my resignation. I don't want to belong to any club that will have me as a member."*

And there's the favorite Groucho-ism of authors: *"Outside of a dog, a book is man's best friend. Inside of a dog, it's too dark to read."*

JERRY SEINFELD

Born in New York in 1954, Jerry Seinfeld brings classic Jewish humor up-to-date. From humble beginnings in comedy clubs to sell-out performances in concert halls, Jerry became a superstar with his TV show **Seinfeld**, in which he creates an extension of his lighthearted social commentary with an attitude and finds humor in the singles life of the big city.

In his stand-up performance and in his book **Seinlanguage**, Jerry examines and exaggerates the comic minutiae of everyday life:

On dating: *"What is a date really, but a job interview that lasts all night?"...* *"God was the first person to fix people up. Fixed up Adam and Eve, you know. I'm sure He said to Adam, 'No, she's nice. She's very free about her body, doesn't wear mch. She was going out with a snake—I think that's over, though.'"*

On pajamas: *"Our pajamas have little lapels, little cuffs, a simulated breast pocket. Do you need a breast pocket on your pajamas? You put a pen in there, you roll over in the middle of the night—you kill yourself!"*

On visualizing parents having sex: *"I mean, sex is a great thing and all, but you don't want to think that your whole life began because somebody had a little too much wine with dinner."*